Exquisite Agony

Books by Nilo Cruz Available from TCG

Ana en el Trópico

Anna in the Tropics

Beauty of the Father

The Color of Desire / Hurricane

Exquisite Agony

Sotto Voce

Two Sisters and a Piano and Other Plays
ALSO INCLUDES:
A Bicycle Country
Capricho
Hortensia and the Museum of Dreams
Lorca in a Green Dress

Exquisite Agony

———◦———

Nilo Cruz

THEATRE COMMUNICATIONS GROUP   NEW YORK   2019

Exquisite Agony is published by Theatre Communications Group, Inc., 520 Eighth Avenue, 24th Floor, New York, NY 10018-4156

"Stranger in the Village," by James Baldwin, originally published in *Harper's Magazine* (1953) and then in *Notes of a Native Son*, Beacon Press (1955).

The publication of *Exquisite Agony* by Nilo Cruz, through TCG's Book Program, is made possible in part by the New York State Council on the Arts with the support of Governor Andrew Cuomo and the New York State Legislature.

Special thanks to the Vilcek Foundation for its generous support of this publication.

TCG books are exclusively distributed to the book trade by Consortium Book Sales and Distribution.

ISBN 978-1-55936- 951-0 (paperback)
ISBN 978-1-55936-913-8 (ebook)
A catalog record for this book is available from the Library of Congress.

Cover, book design and composition by Lisa Govan
Cover image by the author
Author photo by Mar Richard Tousignant

First Edition, December 2019

*People are trapped in history
and history is trapped in them.*

—*James Baldwin*

Exquisite Agony

Production History

Exquisita Agonía (*Exquisite Agony*) was commissioned by and had its world premiere at Repertorio Español (René Buch, Founding Artistic Director; Robert Weber Federico, Executive Producer) in New York City on May 29, 2018, through a Rockefeller Foundation grant. It was directed by José Zayas. The scenic design was by Raúl Abrego, the costume design was by Fernando Then, the lighting design was by Manuel Da Silva, the sound design was by Rafael López, the subtitles were by Edna Lee Figueroa; the stage manager was María Ortiz Poveda. The cast was:

DOCTOR CASTILLO	Germán Jaramillo
MILLIE MARCEL	Luz Nicolás
AMÉR	Gilberto Gabriel Díaz Flores
IMANOL	Pedro De León
ROMY	Soraya Padrao
TOMMY	Gonzalo Trigueros

Characters

DOCTOR CASTILLO: A charismatic man in his fifties, from Latin America. He is cultivated in the classics, in literature, and philosophy, and is a fan of classical music and opera. His duties and devotion toward his patients have increased over the years, along with the evolution of moral consciousness, and the need to have an open heart.

MILLIE MARCEL: An elegant woman in her fifties, born in Latin America, but raised in the United States. She is graceful and exuberant. Her gaze reveals her innermost being, her need to live life to the fullest. She has been woken from a long dream, and is desperate to restore meaning to her life.

AMÉR: A young and genuinely sensitive man in his mid-twenties, from Latin America. He has a delicate face, full of tenderness, which invites warmth and honest smiles. He is nimble and artful, reflective, and almost too wise for the world. You never know what he's brooding about because he has a secret.

IMANOL: A young man in his late twenties, from Latin America. He is Amér's older brother, a knowing city boy, physically built, with masculine and brusque movements that hide his sensibility. He adores his brother and is willing to do anything for him.

ROMY: A young woman in her mid-twenties, from the United States. She is Millie's troubled daughter. Her nature and her looks are rebellious. She is sensitive to the seductions of goth music, and has a bohemian lifestyle. She wears a nose ring, blue lipstick, and has blue highlights in her onyx black hair, which gives her a bluish halo. You would never think that beneath the rebellious veneer there is an unfailing generosity of spirit and goodness.

TOMMY: A young man in his late twenties, from the United States. He is Millie's unbalanced son. He appears to be detached and independent, but he is really a wounded deer. He has strayed far away from his relatives because he prefers to make his family and the world responsible for his problems. Deep inside he has a loving heart, but prefers to show his severity.

TIME

The beginning of autumn.

PLACE

Somewhere in the United States.

SETTING

Various locations such as a doctor's office at a hospital, a simple apartment where Amér is staying with his brother, and Millie's mansion.

Act One

—◀◉▶—

SCENE I

A Cure for Sorrow

A doctor's office. Millie is sitting in a chair by a desk. Doctor Castillo enters and reads her name from a chart.

DOCTOR CASTILLO: Millie Marcel?
MILLIE: Yes, I'm Millie Marcel.

   (Doctor Castillo shakes her hand.)

DOCTOR CASTILLO: Glad to meet you. I'm Doctor Castillo.
MILLIE: Good to meet you, Doctor.

   (He looks at the information on the chart.)

DOCTOR CASTILLO: I admire your voice, Ms. Marcel. I've heard you sing many times. I happened to be in New York last year when you sang at the Met.

MILLIE: That might be the last time I sing from the Massenet repertoire.

DOCTOR CASTILLO: It would be a loss for Massenet.

So what brings you here today, Ms. Marcel?

MILLIE: As you can see, I didn't fill out the form I was given.

DOCTOR CASTILLO: Yes, I noticed.

MILLIE: I'm not ill. I'm here because I thought you could help me with another matter. It has to do with my husband.

DOCTOR CASTILLO: Is he a patient of mine?

MILLIE: No. Not really. I mean . . . you didn't deal with him directly when he was alive.

DOCTOR CASTILLO: Oh, I'm sorry . . . I didn't . . .

MILLIE: I was given your name. I was told my husband's heart was used in a heart transplant that you performed.

DOCTOR CASTILLO: That's possible.

MILLIE *(With hesitation)*: I'm here . . . I'm here . . . because I would like . . . I'd like to meet in person the recipient . . . the patient who received my husband's heart. Do you think that's possible?

DOCTOR CASTILLO: There's a procedure for all of this, Ms. Marcel.

MILLIE: Yes, I . . . I know. The coordinator told me.

DOCTOR CASTILLO: Then you know it takes time.

MILLIE: I know. But I thought . . .

DOCTOR CASTILLO: The meeting of recipients with families of donors is a very sensitive matter. It's not like befriending someone via email or through Facebook.

MILLIE: Yes, I'm aware of that. But I thought . . . I thought maybe you could help me out and speed up the process.

DOCTOR CASTILLO: No, Ms. Marcel. I can't guarantee you that the recipient who got your husband's heart will want to meet you in person. Have you tried contacting the recipient through the transplant coordinator?

MILLIE: I did. I sent the recipient a letter. But I had no luck.

DOCTOR CASTILLO: Sometimes that happens. Many transplant recipients are trying to adapt to a new lifestyle.

MILLIE: I understand. But I also thought that maybe . . . that somehow . . .

DOCTOR CASTILLO: That the patient would like to reach out . . . ?

MILLIE: Yes . . . that maybe . . .

DOCTOR CASTILLO: Not necessarily, Ms. Marcel.

MILLIE: They have been offered a gift . . .

DOCTOR CASTILLO: That's right. And that doesn't mean they're ungrateful . . .

MILLIE: Oh, I'm sure they're not . . .

DOCTOR CASTILLO: But some of them might be experiencing a series of concerns.

MILLIE: Concerns? What kind of concerns?

DOCTOR CASTILLO: Well, there's always the possibility that the heart they have received would reject them or vice versa. Reducing the body's rejection to new tissue is one major barrier to transplantation that we always try to overcome. The physical structure of a person or an animal is . . . how can I explain . . . ? It is xenophobic by nature. And we also have to remember that the transplanted heart isn't just placed in a new body; it receives many other things, a new brain, a new skin, a new home, a new family, and new friends. And whatever else comes with life.

MILLIE: I'd like to know that new body, that new home, that new family. So what do you suggest I do?

DOCTOR CASTILLO: Write to the recipient again.

MILLIE: And is there any other way . . . ? Could you help me out with this matter? . . .

DOCTOR CASTILLO: No. I'm afraid you have to follow the protocol. And as you are well aware, you cannot write to the patient directly.

MILLIE: I know. And to ensure confidentiality, the transplant coordinator will have to review the letter. I know. —All of this is so impersonal. Can't you contact him directly?

DOCTOR CASTILLO: Don't ask me to be biased or exhibit favoritism, Ms. Marcel. If I do this for you, I would have to do it for others. And my priority here is to safeguard my patient's privacy.

MILLIE: I would think the recipient would want to know more about the person who donated his heart.

DOCTOR CASTILLO: No. Not always. I've seen cases in which some recipients would much rather believe that a brand-new heart has been given to them. They don't want to know that the heart belonged to someone else. And then there are other patients who want to know as much as they can about the donor. It is a delicate matter. And you, Ms. Marcel, you also need to protect your identity, especially someone like you who is famous.

(Millie stays lost in thought.)

MILLIE: I assume the recipient . . . this patient, is a man.

DOCTOR CASTILLO: Not necessarily. For a heart transplant the gender of the recipient or the donor is of no importance. What matters are the dimensions of the heart.

(Suddenly, she thinks of her husband's heart in the body of another woman and tears mist her eyes.)

MILLIE: I . . . I . . .

DOCTOR CASTILLO: Does that concern you, Ms. Marcel?

MILLIE: No. No. If it's a woman, then she's lucky, because he had a good heart. Can you find out?

DOCTOR CASTILLO: Yes, I can. What was your husband's full name?

MILLIE: Michael Lorenzo. But everyone called him Lorenzo. *(The name causes her to close her eyes and drown her emotion)* —I'm sorry.

DOCTOR CASTILLO: Are you all right?

MILLIE: Yes. I'm fine. It's been difficult. But I'm fine. Sometimes the days seem identical without him. One day after another, with no change added. Just his absence. But I try to find him in others who knew him. In our daughter and son. In our mutual friends. They always feel like an extension of him.

DOCTOR CASTILLO: Can I ask you a question? Why is it so important for you to meet this person?

MILLIE: Have you ever lost a loved one, Doctor?

DOCTOR CASTILLO: Yes, I can say that I have.

MILLIE: Then you know that it's like losing a part of yourself . . . a part of you as important as your childhood.

DOCTOR CASTILLO: Let me do a little investigating, Ms. Marcel.

MILLIE: Please do. Can I give you the letter so you can send it to the recipient? The coordinator was not as kind as you are.

(She looks for the letter in her handbag.)

DOCTOR CASTILLO: I'll do my best to get it to the person.

(She hands him the letter.)

Just know that you won't get an answer right away. And I can't promise you anything.

13

MILLIE: Thank you.

(She gets up to leave. He rises to his feet out of courtesy.
    As she walks out, he stays looking at the letter in his
hand.)

Scene 2

A Letter from Millie Marcel

Millie is bathed in a pool of light. A spotlight reveals Amér, the recipient, reading the letter.

MILLIE:

Dear Recipient,

May I write to you? Out of a sense of duty or a desire to get to know you, I am putting pen to paper to introduce myself. My name is Millie and I am the wife of the man whose heart you have received. I hope his gift will serve you well in life. I, in turn, am pleased and grateful that you have given a part of him a new existence. I hope we can

15

meet in person one day, that is, when the time is right for you.

Sincerely,

Millie

(Amér, pensively, stays looking at the letter, as the pool of light fades around Millie.)

AMÉR *(Reading from the postscript)*:

P.S. If you would like to write me back, please send your letter to the transplant coordinator and the letter will be forwarded to me.

(Imanol, a handsome young man, enters. He is Amér's older brother.)

IMANOL: I'm going to Roberto's house.

AMÉR: Would you drive me to the library?

IMANOL: When are you going to start driving again? The doctor said you could drive.

AMÉR: I know he did.

IMANOL: Then drive. We have a car.

AMÉR: I get anxious.

IMANOL: Anxious about what?

AMÉR: Driving. Traffic. And getting into an accident.

IMANOL: You need to overcome that.

AMÉR: I know. But after the surgery I feel a strange sensation every time I get inside a car.

IMANOL: It's all in your head.

AMÉR: I think I want to get a bike to get around.

IMANOL: Then you'll end up dead. Drivers have no respect for cyclists in this city.

(Amér draws his attention to the letter in his hand.)

AMÉR: I got a letter from the donor's wife. She wants to meet me in person.

IMANOL: And do you want to meet her?

AMÉR: No.

IMANOL: And why does she want to meet you?

AMÉR: I don't know. Maybe because . . . maybe because I have something that belonged to her husband. Who knows? Maybe she wants me to thank her. Or maybe she wants to thank me.

IMANOL: Thank you for what?

AMÉR: I guess for keeping the man's heart beating.

IMANOL: Nonsense! If anybody should be thankful it's you. The guy is dead. —Give me the letter.

(Amér gives him the letter. Imanol reads.)

AMÉR: She sounds like a nice lady.

IMANOL: Write her back.

AMÉR: And tell her what?

IMANOL: That you'd like to meet her.

AMÉR: No.

IMANOL: You don't want to seem ungrateful.

AMÉR: I don't think I am ready.

IMANOL *(Gives him back the letter)*: Think about it. If it weren't for him perhaps you wouldn't be alive.

AMÉR: Yes, I know.

(Imanol puts his arm around his brother's shoulders and looks at him with tenderness.)

IMANOL: We should write her back. You want me to respond to her letter?

AMÉR: I'd like to forget about everything that's happened to me.

IMANOL: But it did happen. And now you're better. —Give me the letter. I'll write her back.

(Amér doesn't give him the letter.)

AMÉR: I said no.
IMANOL: You're acting like a coward.

(Imanol goes out. Amér puts his hand on his chest and speaks with his heart.)

AMÉR: Can you hear me? What do you think of all this? Why write to her? Why encourage the past? Maybe I shouldn't ask you or myself these questions. If I consult about these things with you, I'd have to take into account your opinion and your will. And who knows where you'd lead me? And if I let myself be guided by you, would I become your servant? No. No. We couldn't live like this. —Let's face it, you've already lived your life and now I have to live mine. You've brought me back to life, but I've also offered you my hands and my eyes, so that you can feel and see the world through them. *(He paces the room)* Shit! Why do I say these things? I never had these thoughts before you lived in my body. The things that go through my mind! Why do I think about all this . . . ? *(Furious)* Why? Who is saying all these things, you or me? No, I'm the one talking. —A heart is not a hero, nor a person, nor a government, nor a country. *(He looks up, his eyes seem lost in the distance)* What is a heart? A port? A bay? A park? A refuge? *(He looks at his arms, at his body, and feels his skin)* No, it's the place where the roads meet . . . like a train station through which fear travels, desire; it's the place that startles me at night . . . from where the chill comes, the panic that strikes me every day. *(He covers his ears)* Enough! Enough! That's where you and I live, where wounds are buried, and embraces are hidden, and debts are redeemed. Therefore, it has to be a free place. And we have to adapt and be courteous to each other.

(The lights shift, signaling a new day.)

Scene 3

The Father

A spacious house, elegantly decorated.

MILLIE *(Offstage)*: Don't cut off any more branches, Berto.

> *(Millie enters, holding a bouquet of eucalyptus branches. Her daughter, Romy, follows, carrying a couple of vases.)*

He's liable to cut down the whole eucalyptus tree if I don't tell him.

ROMY: We could live with fewer shrubs.

> *(They place the branches and vases on the table. They begin to cut the stems of the branches, placing the eucalyptus branches inside the vases.)*

MILLIE: We're not living downtown where everything is barren and cemented.

ROMY: At least they don't have raccoons and opossums.

MILLIE: You hate that I leave food for the opossums.

ROMY: They're ugly rats with big teeth that carry diseases.

MILLIE: Indeed, they are ugly little creatures. That's why I feel sorry for them, because no one likes them. But it's the squirrels you like to feed that actually carry rabies.

ROMY: Squirrels or whatever . . . we're not running a zoo, Mother.

MILLIE: I know we're not. But these animals have a right to live.

ROMY: And they have a right not to suffer. But if we continue to feed them and allow them to live in the city, where they're exposed to the traffic of cars, then they're doomed. The other night we killed a raccoon, Tommy and I.

MILLIE: Romy!!!

ROMY: We killed it out of mercy, Mother. It had just been hit by another car and it was wobbling, disoriented. I told Tommy to stop the car so I could at least guide it to the side of the road, so it could maybe regain its strength and get on with its life. But the poor thing was quivering and the sound it was making was so awful that I went back to the car and told Tommy to finish him off and end its misery. And we did. We gave it the final blow. And I think it was grateful that we ended its agony.

MILLIE: Romy. That's awful. Why did you tell me this?

ROMY: Because sometimes we have to put an end to misery.

MILLIE: Do you think I like to dwell on misery?

ROMY: No, I suspect you're stuck, Mother. And you know it. You're obsessed with Father's death.

MILLIE: It's barely a year since he died.

ROMY: And you need to get on with your life.

MILLIE: I'm doing better.

ROMY: Then the pills you're taking must be helping.

MILLIE: I don't take them anymore.

ROMY: Humph! I suspected that much.

MILLIE: Grieving is necessary, Romy.

ROMY: Yes, but not the way you grieve.

MILLIE: Imagine a world without sadness.

ROMY: It would be a joyful world.

MILLIE: Then we wouldn't be able to value happiness.

ROMY: Your concept of contrast is too vast and extreme.

MILLIE: We're not all supposed to react to tragedy the same way.

ROMY: Precisely. But we must also learn to move on.

MILLIE: But I am. I am. I am moving on . . . slowly. I wrote a letter to the person who has received your father's heart.

ROMY: That's not moving on, Mother. Let Father die! Let him die, Mother! You're still keeping him alive. Put him to rest.

MILLIE: I think it will help me if I talk to this person. I think it will do me much good if I meet him.

ROMY: Do you know who it is?

MILLIE: No.

(Millie laughs. She walks away.)

ROMY: And how come you assume it's a man? . . .

MILLIE: Because I know.

ROMY: Mamá, it could be an old lady in need of a heart.

MILLIE: God forbid. I know it's a man.

ROMY: And how do you know, Mother?

MILLIE: I know so. I sense it. Besides, his heart wouldn't do well in an old lady's chest. It'd be trying to jump out every time she takes a breath.

(They both laugh.)

ROMY: He wouldn't do well either in a butcher's body.

MILLIE: No, not your dad. —Painters, archaeologists, pilots, would've been good recipients for him.

ROMY: So elitist, Mother!

MILLIE: I am. I want the best for your father.

ROMY: Well, that's not the way it's done. His heart could've ended up in the body of a killer, a gigolo, a thief, or a porn star, and we have to accept that.

MILLIE: Ay, Romy, for God's sake!

ROMY: It's the truth. Otherwise, you're being selective and that defeats the whole purpose of giving someone a second chance in life.

MILLIE: All right. Delete. Delete thought. Let's think positive. Reset computer. Username: Bright side. Password: Blue skies. If his skin is purple, red, yellow, black, we will accept him . . . if he's from Turkmenistan, France, India, we will also embrace him.

ROMY *(Touches her mother's face and kisses her)*: You really want Father to come back, don't you?

MILLIE: He hasn't left.

ROMY: Why is it you love him so much, when he wasn't always good to you?

MILLIE: Because one should always love without boundaries.

ROMY: Do you think Father loved you that way?

MILLIE: I think he did in his reckless way. He would always come back because he couldn't live without me.

ROMY: Let's do something. I'll write a letter to this young man, and maybe we can get him to meet us.

MILLIE: Let's have a drink.

ROMY: Oh, Mother! You'll need another password for that.

MILLIE: All right. No tears.

ROMY: And username?
MILLIE: Onwards.

(The two women gather their things, preparing to leave for a night out.)

Scene 4

A Letter from Amér

Amér and Imanol enter. They begin to write a letter.

AMÉR:

> Dear Millie,
>   I received your letter yesterday, and I am happy
> that you wrote to me.

IMANOL: Write your name but not your last name.

AMÉR:

> My name is Amér. I have been recovering from my
> surgery these past few months and I'm doing much
> better. My brother has been kind enough to accom-

pany me here from my country for the surgery. We are staying at the apartment of my father's friend.

IMANOL: Write that you can hardly write thank you . . .

AMÉR:

I can hardly write thank you . . .

IMANOL:

. . . because that is not enough to express how grateful I am.

AMÉR: All right.
IMANOL: Tell her that you're willing to meet with her.
AMÉR: I'm not going to write that.
IMANOL: Of course you will
AMÉR: No. I'm not going to meet with her.
IMANOL: Meet the woman, for God's sake!
AMÉR: I said no.
IMANOL: Then figure out what to write, and show her some kindness.

(Imanol gets irritated and moves away from him.)

AMÉR:

Although I would like to meet you, I'm afraid it will be impossible . . .

IMANOL: Don't write that, for God's sake!
AMÉR: Then what?

IMANOL:

Although I would like to meet you, and the heart your husband has given me would like to be near you once again . . .

AMÉR: You're crazy!

(Amér shakes his head in disapproval.)

I'm not going to write that!
IMANOL: Why not?
AMÉR: Because it sounds ridiculous!
IMANOL: All right. All right. Just don't be clumsy.

(Amér thinks about it for a moment . . .)

AMÉR:

I still don't feel like myself.

(Looks at his brother. Imanol nods.)

My mind is cloudy and I don't quite yet know who
I am.

*(Looks at his brother. Imanol is not fully convinced but
Amér continues.)*

This might have to do with the medication I am
taking, which helps my body not to reject the gift
your husband has given me.

*(Looks at his brother. Imanol offers a gentle smile, feeling
and showing empathy for his brother.)*

I'm still trying to get used to the sounds that make
what is now my heart jump, like the restless rush
of car tires, the speed of flying airplanes, and even
the flood of people's voices.

(Imanol is impacted by this line and tears well up in his eyes.)

> I need to live inward at the moment, so that I can heal myself, then I could live outwardly again. I hope you understand why it is difficult for me to meet you at the present moment.
>   Sincerely,
>   Amér

(Imanol pats his brother on the shoulder.)

IMANOL: Good job. I'll drop it off at the mailbox.

(Amér hands the letter to Imanol, as the lights reveal Millie holding and responding to the letter that has been delivered by the post.)

MILLIE:
> Dear Amér,
>   I salute you with a greeting hand. I'm very sorry that you won't be able to meet with me. But all you wrote in your letter found a place and a resonant sound within me. I do realize it is too early for you to see me. For the time being, let us prepare one another for this encounter. I invite you to write me at length and allow me to acquaint myself with you through your letters. Tell me what you like to do most in life. What are your hobbies? What films, what books have stayed with you? If we get to know each other, if we send fragments of ourselves in letters, our meeting will be less awkward when it finally happens. I wave goodbye to you for now.
>   Millie

Scene 5

Advice from a Doctor

The doctor's office. Amér is wearing a hospital gown. Doctor Castillo uses a stethoscope to listen to Amér's heart. Imanol is in the room for the examination.

DOCTOR CASTILLO: Any shortness of breath?
AMÉR: No.
DOCTOR CASTILLO: Any fever?
AMÉR: No.
DOCTOR CASTILLO: Any fatigue?
AMÉR: No.
DOCTOR CASTILLO: Sore throat? Cold sores?
AMÉR: No.

DOCTOR CASTILLO: Then we're making progress. All the lab results look good. The endomyocardial biopsies don't show any cellular rejection.

IMANOL: Amér, do you want to tell him how you feel sometimes?

(Amér vacillates.)

DOCTOR CASTILLO: Is there something you should tell me, Amér?

AMÉR: No, I . . . I think it's just the medication I'm taking.

DOCTOR CASTILLO: What is it, Amér?

AMÉR: I . . . I have . . . I've been a little depressed.

IMANOL: Depressed or anxious?

AMÉR: Overwhelmed, Doctor.

DOCTOR CASTILLO: All of these feelings are to be expected. We went over this.

IMANOL: But it's more than that. Why don't you tell him, Amér?

AMÉR: Well, I . . . I feel very sad.

DOCTOR CASTILLO: And what makes you feel sad?

AMÉR: I don't know. I can't describe it . . .

IMANOL: Didn't you say you felt a sort of guilt?

AMÉR: Yes.

DOCTOR CASTILLO: And what sort of guilt is that?

AMÉR: Is it right to say that it has to do with what I lost?

IMANOL: You didn't lose anything. That's what I keep telling him, Doctor!

AMÉR *(Harshly)*: I lost my heart!

IMANOL: It didn't serve you!

AMÉR: I lived with it for a long time!

IMANOL: All right, I'm leaving. I'm fed up with him.

DOCTOR CASTILLO *(Trying to control them)*: Boys! Boys! That is not necessary. *(To Amér)* Everything that you're feeling is part of the cycle of adjustment.

AMÉR: Even when I feel palpitations? Even when my heart beats desperately, loudly, as if to burst out of my body?

DOCTOR CASTILLO: That could be anxiety.

IMANOL: Tell him what's going on . . .

AMÉR: It's okay, Imanol . . . I'm fine . . . I'm fine . . .

IMANOL: The doctor needs to know.

DOCTOR CASTILLO: What is it, Amér?

IMANOL: He's acting strange. He's been talking . . .

AMÉR: . . . I can tell him. You don't have to speak for me.

(Amér lowers his head. He looks up again. He speaks as though detached from himself:)

Sometimes I sit in the dark of my room and talk to the man whose heart I got.

DOCTOR CASTILLO: And what do you tell him?

AMÉR *(A burst of contained emotion)*: I tell him to please go away . . . to go away . . . to go away . . .

DOCTOR CASTILLO *(Calming him)*: Amér . . . Amér . . . shhhh . . . It's okay.

IMANOL: Are you afraid?

AMÉR: No. Not of him. I fear that I am not myself anymore. I feel I've been divided, that something foreign lives within me. And I have strange thoughts.

DOCTOR CASTILLO: Such as?

AMÉR: I . . . I don't know . . . I . . . I wonder if this person whose heart I got would've liked me in life . . . Or if I would've chosen him as a friend.

(Doctor Castillo turns to Imanol, trying to find an answer.)

IMANOL: He's been having nightmares.

AMÉR: No, they're not nightmares. They're just strange dreams.

DOCTOR CASTILLO: And what did you dream about?

31

(No answer.)

Tell us. We'd like to know.

AMÉR *(Not giving the dream any importance. Agitated)*: Nothing important . . . I was at a store . . . but it wasn't an ordinary store. It really was an insignificant dream.

DOCTOR CASTILLO: What kind of store was it?

AMÉR: It was . . . *(A grimace. Distance, remembering)* It was more like a market . . . a place that sold hearts. And each heart had a description of the person it had belonged to. And there was a heart that caught my attention.

DOCTOR CASTILLO: What was different about it?

AMÉR: It was the heart of an actor.

DOCTOR CASTILLO: And you wanted that heart for you?

AMÉR: No. I was looking for mine. My own heart. *(He smiles, chuckles)* And can you believe it? There was an area of unwanted hearts . . .

DOCTOR CASTILLO: And yours was there?

AMÉR: I looked for it in the pile. *(Smiles)* It turned out their value had been reduced because they had belonged to people who were not good, like killers and thieves.

DOCTOR CASTILLO: And yours wasn't there, of course.

AMÉR: No . . .

DOCTOR CASTILLO: And was there a heart from the store you wanted for yourself?

AMÉR: Maybe the heart of the actor.

DOCTOR CASTILLO: And what was it about that heart that appealed to you?

AMÉR: I don't know. It occurred to me that the actor's heart would want to get to know me. Actors study people and their hearts. I thought it'd be sensitive to me and it would probably want to study and interpret someone like me. *(In a delirium)* —I don't know, Doctor. I don't know. I'm confused . . . I'm confused . . . I am so confused. I'm confused . . . I don't know . . . I don't know if it's the medicine. What did you do to me? What did you do? *(He moves away from them)* What have you done to me? What have you done?

DOCTOR CASTILLO *(Trying to calm him)*: Amér, listen to me.

IMANOL: Amér, don't get that way!

DOCTOR CASTILLO *(Trying to encourage him)*: Amér, in an ideal world, a store of hearts would be a good thing to have. But hearts last a period of four hours out of the body, so we don't have the luxury to ask for personal descriptions to find the heart that would match the recipient. We look for other things in hearts to match the patient with the donor.

AMÉR: But as patients . . . as recipients . . . Are we liable to inherit personal traits from our donors?

DOCTOR CASTILLO: No.

AMÉR: And is that something you have been able to determine? . . . Because I feel . . . I feel . . .

DOCTOR CASTILLO: I think you're just a very sensitive and imaginative young man.

AMÉR *(Defiantly)*: No. Is there a possibility—?

DOCTOR CASTILLO: No, there's no scientific evidence.

AMÉR: But I searched . . . I searched for information and I found things written about it.

DOCTOR CASTILLO: Yes, there are patients who have reported having changes in food taste or in their style of dress, and even perceiving sensations that might pertain to their donors. But that doesn't mean . . .

IMANOL: Then that's what he's feeling.

DOCTOR CASTILLO: No. I wouldn't rush to any conclusions. These could be lingering symptoms of his illness. They could also be side effects of his trauma.

AMÉR: What if they were memories of the donor?

DOCTOR CASTILLO: And how would we know, Amér?

AMÉR: These sensations feel foreign to me.

IMANOL: What do you think, Doctor?

DOCTOR CASTILLO: There are books out there that talk about these memories, and they contain testimonies of patients. But this discourse is often met with strong denial in my profession.

IMANOL: And why is that?

DOCTOR CASTILLO: Because the idea of a heart containing memories is difficult for a scientist or a clinician to accept. And my scientific thinking doesn't allow me to accept this.

AMÉR: And how about your own heart?

DOCTOR CASTILLO: Amér, consider this, what would the brain do if the heart engages in the thinking process?

AMÉR: It . . . it . . . I believe it would do what it always does. But the heart does think, Doctor.

DOCTOR CASTILLO: We are not talking about a sentient or romantic heart, as the poets have described it in poems and sonnets.

AMÉR: But the heart doesn't forget to be a heart; it recognizes itself and everything around it.

DOCTOR CASTILLO: Yes, when it comes to its function in the body. It has biological instructions, which have to do with genetics. Ancestral instructions. And genes are the most obedient rememberers. The heart validates its nature just like the brain and every other part of the body. It has a magnificent force, which doesn't forget how powerful it is in the body and that's the extent of its memory. *(Points to his brain and taps it playfully)* Just know that the brain is the one that's tricky; it makes us imagine things that are not there. —I advise you not to dwell on this.

AMÉR *(Nods)*: Thank you, Doctor.

DOCTOR CASTILLO: Very good then. Let me know if you want to meet the donor's wife.

(Doctor Castillo rises to his feet and pats Amér on the shoulder.)

Be kind to yourself.

(Doctor Castillo goes out, followed by Imanol.
Amér stays motionless, thinking. His prostration is indescribable.)

Scene 6

Letters from Amér and Romy

Amér, in his hospital robe, recites a letter he has written. He disrobes in front of a mirror and studies his scar. Music plays: Mahler's Symphony No. 3, What the Angels Tells Me.

AMÉR:

Dear Millie,

I've been trying to make peace with myself and be more accepting of my new life and of those like you, who come with this new existence. Today when I was reading a book, I realized I like to read used books not only because a story is about to unfold, but they also possess the fingerprints, the coffee stains of those who have read them . . . It pleases me to know that books are passed from hand to hand, to remind us that their words serve a useful purpose in life, which brings me to the subject of your husband Lorenzo and his heart. I find myself thinking of him often, and spending time with him in more ways than one. From inside my body, I take Lorenzo for walks, hum tunes, and wonder how he saw the world. He's a companion who demands music and light. Two questions: Did he like eating honey and cheese? Did he like almonds? I find that I'm always craving these things. I look forward to meeting you and your daughter.

(He puts on a red sweater.
Romy is revealed in a pool of light, reciting a letter.)

ROMY:

Dear Amér,

I have read the letters you have sent my mother, which I found very touching. I do hope you decide to meet with us. It's strange, even though I haven't met you in person, I dreamt of you continuously last night. You were wearing a red sweater and you were taking a bike ride in the afternoon. Your hands were gripping the handlebars, and your feet were circling the pedals toward me. And I could hear the tires turning on the pavement at a high speed. I was resting on the grass under the shade of a tree. From there I could hear your bicycle singing in my direction. And when you stopped before me, you offered to give me a ride. And as we chased the last rays of the sun, the night chased us, and we got lost on a dirt road. I want to believe that one day we might be able to ride a bicycle, as I used to with my father. Do you have a bike? If you don't, we have one. Do you even know how to ride a bicycle? Come meet us.

Yours,
Romy

SCENE 7

Lorenzo Always

The doctor's office. Amér and Imanol enter.

IMANOL: There is no one here.

AMÉR: It's lunchtime.

IMANOL: I bet you the meeting is at the chapel.

AMÉR: They told me to meet here first.

IMANOL: And why do they want us to go to the chapel?

AMÉR: I don't know. Maybe so the meeting would be something sacred.

IMANOL: And what are you going to say to Millie when you see her?

AMÉR: I don't know. I haven't thought about it.

IMANOL: You have to talk about something.

AMÉR: I'll know what to tell her when I see her.

IMANOL: Are you going to tell her what's been happening to you?

AMÉR: I don't know her well enough to tell her.

IMANOL: Whatever.

AMÉR: What would you do?

IMANOL: I'd look for a moment to close my eyes and let her talk to him and tell him whatever she wants.

AMÉR: So suddenly?

IMANOL: Well, it'd be an invitation to let her feel close to him.

AMÉR: And what would you say?

IMANOL: I do not know, something like . . . Nothing comes to mind.

AMÉR: What if I say something like . . . ? I know you've been looking for him for a long time . . .

IMANOL: That sounds good.

AMÉR: And she might answer, "Yes, for a long time."

IMANOL: Then you can say, "Is this what you dreamt about?"

AMÉR: And I imagine that she'll remain silent.

IMANOL: She might. I don't suppose there'll be any words. But maybe she'll want to hug you and kiss you.

AMÉR: And what do I do if that happens?

IMANOL: Let her kiss you. There's nothing wrong with that.

AMÉR: Of course. It'd seem strange to me . . .

IMANOL: What? Closing your eyes and letting yourself go?

AMÉR: It is not just about closing your eyes.

IMANOL: What is it to you? Why can't you give in and succumb to the moment?

AMÉR: I'm not like you.

IMANOL: Want to find out what it would be like?

AMÉR: Forget it.

IMANOL: No. Close your eyes. Close them. *(Amér closes his eyes)* She walks over to you and asks, "How can I talk to you?"

AMÉR: And what do I tell her?

IMANOL: What she would like to hear, certain words.

AMÉR: Such as?

IMANOL: That he listens to her. That he remembers her.

AMÉR: How does he remember her?

IMANOL: As in a photograph he had of her.

AMÉR: What photo?

IMANOL: I don't know. Make up something. A picture of her on the beach. The one where she's standing by the shore of the sea.

AMÉR: What if she asks if I remember that day?

IMANOL: You would have to invent the sea. The day the photo was taken. It would be an old photo so that it doesn't look like a specific sea. Even she herself will tell you that the sea can never be concrete.

AMÉR: And what do I tell her then?

IMANOL: I do not know, that the sea should never be confined, that it should be boundless like the love she feels for Lorenzo.

(Imanol kisses him. Amér opens his eyes.)

AMÉR: What are you doing?

IMANOL: So that you practice.

(Amér wipes his mouth. Imanol laughs.)

AMÉR: Don't make fun of me.

IMANOL: I'm only teaching you.

AMÉR: How do you manage to talk like that?

IMANOL: Experience. Life. You'll do well, little brother.

AMÉR: I'm so nervous, as if I were getting married.

IMANOL: Come on. Do not worry.

(Music. As Imanol and Amér are about to leave, Romy enters and stops for a moment in front of the brothers. Their eyes meet under the light that seems to be stripped naked when a cloud passes by.

Everything begins with this moment.

Now everything acquires a suspenseful color.

Romy breaks the lapse of time and walks toward a chair. Amér turns and stays looking at her. Imanol takes Amér by the arm, guiding him toward the door. They exit the doctor's office.

Romy stays looking at everything around her, feeling a strange sensation.

Tommy enters and goes to his sister.)

TOMMY: Where is mamá?

ROMY: She is talking to the coordinator.

TOMMY: Are we meeting here?

ROMY: The doctor thought it'd be best to come here first.

TOMMY: Mother told me to go to the hospital chapel . . . I was waiting there like a dummy.

ROMY: She wants everyone to meet there first, and then we can all head over to the house and have dinner.

TOMMY: What does she think this is, a wedding? A funeral?

ROMY: You know Mother!

TOMMY: I was ready to leave.

ROMY: They're late. The doctor was running late with a patient.

TOMMY: And the guy?

ROMY: I don't know. We have no way of getting in touch with him.

TOMMY: Maybe he chickened out.

ROMY: Then she'll be very upset. She prepared a meal.

TOMMY: Without knowing the guy?

ROMY: Those are her plans.

TOMMY: Is that why you're all dressed up?

ROMY: Mother told me to dress up. I didn't want to. But I wanted to please her.

(Millie, wearing an elegant dress, enters and sees Tommy.)

MILLIE: Tommy, you're here.

TOMMY: Look at you. You look like a merry widow.

MILLIE: And what did you want me to wear—mourning clothes? *(She kisses him)*

TOMMY *(Gently)*: Well, you're not going out on a date.

MILLIE: I know I'm not. *(Playfully)* But one should always tempt fate.

TOMMY *(Laughing)*: What fate, Mother?

MILLIE: Oh, I'm kidding. I just want to be presentable.

TOMMY *(Toying with her)*: Presentable for a young man who has your husband's heart?

MILLIE: That's not funny.

TOMMY: Then what are you referring to? A simple meeting with Father and not the boy?

MILLIE *(With delight)*: Oh, if that were the case I'd put on the black Yves Saint Laurent dress, the one I wore at the last concert I did with your father. —Oh, don't look at me with those eyes. Why don't we drink a little hot chocolate downstairs? It sweetens the soul and calms the nerves.

TOMMY: I'm not nervous. We are not expecting the president.

MILLIE: Oh, why did you come here if you're going to start acting like that? You're such a clown.

TOMMY *(With tenderness)*: Mom, your behavior is a bit frightening.

MILLIE: Oh Tommy, I would've thought that you of all people would recognize the importance of this meeting.

TOMMY: Please, don't tell me you're suggesting complicity now.

MILLIE: I don't know whom you take after, Tommy.

ROMY: Yes, we have a clash of personalities in this family.

MILLIE: Exactly. I have personality and you're still developing yours.

TOMMY *(Laughing)*: No, Mother. Your notion of this encounter is absurdly romantic.

MILLIE: Well, I can't help it if my capacity for loving far exceeds your notion of romance.

(She takes out her powder compact from her purse and powders her face.)

TOMMY: It's a morbid obsession, Mother, and you know it. *(As if she were a child)* I know you. If it were up to you, you would've kept Daddy's heart in a case, like those churches in Europe . . . the ones that preserve the remains of saints in reliquaries.

MILLIE *(Laughing)*: Yes. I'm Catholic and your father was a saint.

TOMMY *(Folds his arm)*: What's in a heart, Mother, after a person is gone?

MILLIE: Plenty. Your father's heart saved a young man.

TOMMY: But the problem is that your grieving has become immoderate and excessive.

MILLIE: And how do you expect me to grieve?

TOMMY: A person can grieve and at the same time hold back. But you . . . you wear yourself out. You indulge yourself.

MILLIE: All right! All right! I'm going out for a smoke.

ROMY: No, you cannot smoke.

MILLIE: And how do you expect me to quit, if he's trying to drive me crazy? Romy, let me smoke. You have my cigarettes.

(Romy pulls out the pack of cigarettes.)

TOMMY: Don't start spoiling her.

MILLIE: Just leave. Go. Go . . .

TOMMY: I'm not going anywhere. You asked me to come and now I'm here.

MILLIE: Then don't torment me like this. Doctor Castillo is going out of his way to do this for me.

TOMMY: Mother, you're not doing yourself any good by doing all this.

MILLIE: If I don't look forward to this, what do I have, Tommy?

TOMMY: You have us. You have a son and a daughter, and soon you'll have a grandchild.

ROMY: She's become selfish.

MILLIE: Me selfish?

ROMY: Yes, you forget that soon I'll need your help when I have the baby.

TOMMY: You have a family who cares for you and needs you! You have your music. Your commitment to an orchestra . . . to your art . . . to people who respect you . . . like Fabio Luisi and Gustavo Dudamel.

MILLIE: I don't want to sing, not with the way I have been feeling, not in the condition I'm in. I have no inspiration.

ROMY: She has canceled all her concerts.

TOMMY: Did you really do that, Mother?

(Millie doesn't answer.)

Did you? You need to get back on the stage again.

MILLIE: I don't need to do anything, Tommy.

TOMMY: Can't you try to find yourself in the music you sing?

MILLIE: And whom would I find? Someone who will resort to an impersonation of who I used to be, so I can recognize myself? No, that would be disastrous. I don't play silly games with myself.

(She pulls out her powder compact again and looks at herself in the mirror.)

TOMMY: But you do, Mother. You do.

MILLIE: How little you know me! *(Laughs quietly)* The other day, here, in this hospital, I laughed at the transplant coordinator who interrogated me. *(She powders her face)* He had the audacity to grill me. He called it screening, but it was plain, appalling, grilling. He wanted to make sure I met the criteria to meet the recipient. He wanted to make sure that I was stable-minded . . . *(Laughs)* As if I were mad. *(Savoring the words with certain irony)* He said I have to be sane and sound before I meet this young man. *(She closes the powder compact)*

TOMMY: Mother, what makes you think this young man is going to change your life?

MILLIE: Because throughout this process I find fragments of Lorenzo and myself. Because after my meeting with the hospital coordinator, I took the lift to the first floor and I remembered that I met Lorenzo in an elevator. Because the obedience of that moment came back. I was alone in the lift, inside the throat of the hospital, and the elevator got stuck in between floors. *(Recalls the moment, relishing in its glory)* And I remained still, in the grip of its cage, between two floors, between two worlds, lost in the memory of Lorenzo . . . and I debated whether to press the alarm and signal to someone that I was trapped, because at that moment I felt that the lift had become your father's arms and he was carrying me close to his chest. *(She shakes her head, returns to the present moment)* —Then the elevator shook. It started descending again, delivering me back to the world. And as the doors opened and I stepped out of its mouth, I realized that was a sign . . . that was a sign to find this young man.

TOMMY *(Tenderly)*: Oh, Mother!

ROMY: I think the doctor is coming.

(Doctor Castillo enters.)

DOCTOR CASTILLO: The coordinator just called. The boys are here. I'll tell my assistant to send them up.

(Doctor Castillo exits. Millie goes for her purse and puts the compact inside. She searches for a small bottle of perfume.)

MILLIE: Please be kind to Amér and his brother.
TOMMY: Oh yes, I'll be very kind. Should I treat them like cousins, too?

(Millie's purse falls on the floor and everything spills out: perfume bottle, powder compact, tissue paper, cell phone, pillbox, etc.)

MILLIE: Oh God! Now look what you made me do!

(Romy helps her mother.)

ROMY: Leave Mother alone!
TOMMY *(Laughing)*: I just loathe how sentimental you've both become.
ROMY: And I hate how bitter and cynical you are!
MILLIE: We can't help it if he feels contempt for his family.

(Tommy kneels down to help them.)

TOMMY: I just don't get this militant sorrow of yours.
MILLIE: Perhaps there's a lesson to be learned.
TOMMY: Then share it with me when you learn it.
MILLIE: I do ask God every day to let me love you without reservation!

(They have placed everything back in the purse, except the cell phone, which Tommy holds in his hand. Romy helps her mother up.)

TOMMY: That's something you don't ask, Mother. That's something you act upon.

MILLIE: And can you apply this practical wisdom toward us?

TOMMY: Here, your phone. Call me. Call me and I'll tell you something.

ROMY: They're here with the doctor.

(Amér walks in wearing a raincoat, even though it is not raining. Imanol and Doctor Castillo follow him. Millie sees Amér, and for a moment, time stands still. The whole room is bathed in a subdued, suspenseful light. For Millie, his presence is a memory, the personification of Lorenzo. She rises to her feet. There is an expression of indescribable joy on her face, as she puts her hand to her heart. For Amér, this encounter feels as if two different times have suddenly met and merged into a single moment, causing him to look for an original reaction, but instead he is dumbfounded. Then, after a moment, Millie advances toward Amér slowly.)

MILLIE: May I hug you?

AMÉR: Yes.

(She embraces him. After a moment they separate and she stays looking at him.)

MILLIE: You are as I imagined you to be. *(To Amér)* You might think I am being too forward . . . and it is somewhat embarrassing to ask you this . . . and please . . . you can

say no . . . but . . . may I listen to his heart? . . . No. Your
heart. —May I?

(Amér looks at Doctor Castillo and then his brother.)

AMÉR: Of course.

*(He unbuttons his shirt. She moves near his naked chest,
and closes her eyes. She smiles after she hears the beating
sound of the heart.)*

MILLIE: I can hear him. To hear him softly. To hear you.

*(Millie withdraws her cheek from his chest. She is deli-
cately stunned. She shakes her head. She lowers her eyes
and then looks up. An inexplicable expression of hope is
now present on her face.)*

Act Two

———◂◦▸———

SCENE I

A Dinner Party

Millie's house. Amér and Imanol enter.

AMÉR: The house is beautiful.

IMANOL: So is the daughter. How do I look?

AMÉR: We're not here to flirt with the daughter.

IMANOL: Then why are we here, to play solitaire? *(He combs his hair)* How do I look?

AMÉR: Ugly. Terrible. And me? Do I look good?

IMANOL: Awful. Dreadful.

AMÉR: You will not win over the daughter.

IMANOL: Who says? *(He unbuttons his shirt)*

AMÉR: I'm telling you. Don't show off. Button up your shirt.

IMANOL: No, it stays open. You're the one who needs to put on the tie I gave you.

AMÉR: And look like a father? Over my dead body!

IMANOL: Come here. Let me fix your collar.

(Romy enters.)

ROMY: Do you want to see the garden?

AMÉR: Yes, the garden . . .

IMANOL *(To himself)*: Sure, the garden . . . your room, the garage, the kitchen, the basement, the attic, the roof . . .

(They leave to explore.
Millie comes in with Doctor Castillo.)

MILLIE: I have always been unconventional. Normalcy kills the artist. Who wants to be average and conventional?

DOCTOR CASTILLO: So you strive to live life more fully?

MILLIE: Doesn't everyone?

DOCTOR CASTILLO: Not necessarily. Not everyone can aspire to have that privilege, especially those who are poor and sick. They don't even have that option. Even the middle class . . . Do we still have a middle class? Nowadays we've been taught to live on credit. We measure our status by our spending entitlement. The more entitled we feel to borrow against the future, the more rights we think we have to live the life enjoyed by the elite. I know I sound like an antiquated observer of existence. But even in medicine, we find remedies, payments of installments against maladies we can't cure. In the end, we all make up our own little world with limitations, even those who are well off.

MILLIE: I'm curious about your life. Don't you get restless?

DOCTOR CASTILLO: Of course, I do.

MILLIE: Don't you want to be part of the life we don't get to see?

DOCTOR CASTILLO: Every day I get to see the life that others don't want to see at the hospital.

MILLIE: I don't mean that kind of life.

DOCTOR CASTILLO *(Playfully)*: Do you think I wear a lab coat everywhere I go?

MILLIE *(Laughs)*: No, of course not.

DOCTOR CASTILLO: Do you think I am always as impersonal as I am, when I wear a stethoscope around my neck?

MILLIE: I don't know. I find you to be very enigmatic.

(He laughs.)

DOCTOR CASTILLO: And if I talk about myself, would I be less enigmatic? Don't you agree that it is better to get to know someone over time?

MILLIE *(Smiling, lowering her eyes)*: Are you saying you wish to know me?

DOCTOR CASTILLO: Let's put it this way. I would miss you very much if I stopped seeing you.

MILLIE: You must feel sorry for me.

DOCTOR CASTILLO: No. I learned in medical school not to feel sorry for those who visit my office; even my patients expect that from me.

MILLIE: Yet you had compassion for me when I visited you.

DOCTOR CASTILLO: The work I do is very different from yours, Ms. Marcel. You are allowed to show your emotions when you sing. You're encouraged to sing from your heart. But we are not allowed to show any feelings when we put on a stethoscope and listen to the most private part of a person. But I've tried to unlearn everything I was taught at school, because each heart has its own biography and ways of revealing its story. That's why I allowed myself to listen to you and respond.

MILLIE: And I am grateful.

DOCTOR CASTILLO: When you're feeling better, I'd like to take you to a concert. No pressure.

MILLIE: I would like that very much.

DOCTOR CASTILLO: Although I'd much rather if it were a concert of you singing. But to sing and attend a concert all at once might be impossible.

MILLIE *(Laughing)*: No. I would have to sing for you.

DOCTOR CASTILLO: I'd be honored.

(Romy enters, followed by Amér, Imanol and Tommy.)

ROMY: It's starting to sprinkle. We brought the snacks inside.

MILLIE: It's probably a passing cloud.

ROMY: No, it looks like there's going to be a downpour.

MILLIE: Oh dear! So much for sitting out in the garden. *(To Amér)* Did you enjoy the tour of the house?

AMÉR: Very much.

DOCTOR CASTILLO: Well, if it's going to rain I'm afraid I'll have to go soon. I still have hospital visits to make.

MILLIE: Oh please, stay a while longer.

DOCTOR CASTILLO: Not much longer.

MILLIE *(To Amér)*: How lucky you are to have found Doctor Castillo.

AMÉR: I am very lucky.

IMANOL: We came all the way from our country because he was highly recommended.

MILLIE: May I take your raincoat?

AMÉR: I prefer to keep it on.

(He stares down at his shoes.)

MILLIE: Are you sure you won't be more comfortable without it?

AMÉR: I'm perfectly comfortable. Thank you. I wear it to protect myself from the draft of air conditioners. I'm always afraid of getting sick. People keep their central air very cold here.

MILLIE: Would you like us to make the temperature warmer?

AMÉR: No, I'm quite all right, señora.

MILLIE: Sit down. Please, sit.

(Amér and Imanol sit on a bench.)

AMÉR: Thank you.

MILLIE: This morning when I was walking my dog, Bingo . . . I named him Bingo, so that every time I call him I think I am winning something . . . Silly me.

DOCTOR CASTILLO: Oh, there's nothing silly about that, Ms. Marcel. I think it's a good thing if it makes you feel like a winner.

MILLIE: Oh, I just gain Bingo's attention, and that always brings me a sense of satisfaction and surprise. —But as I was walking Bingo today, I thought of instinct, about what goes into its makeup. I thought of how Bingo's ears prick up and he becomes attentive when he hears a bird and gets ready to hunt it down. I'm referring to the genetic alertness that's been passed on to him. And I thought of my own fervor in life to create sound and music. How musical talent was passed on to me and to others in my family.

TOMMY: What are you trying to get at, Mother?

MILLIE: Oh, I'm talking about how things get passed on, instinct, grace, and physical appearance.

TOMMY: Yes, we got that.

MILLIE *(Bothered by his response)*: Tommy. I just question whether they're passed on to us through inherent memory.

TOMMY: Through genes, Mother. Our DNA. Everybody knows that.

MILLIE: You're not listening to what I'm saying!

TOMMY: Yes, I am, Mother.

MILLIE: What I'm talking about is the divine order and will that doesn't allow water to be anything else but water . . . or the force of nature that decrees that a leaf not forget to be anything other than a leaf . . . And then I wonder about the hybridization of flowers? How a new hybridized flower contains colors and traits of two other flowers. And I just wonder . . . I mean, I question if there's something of my husband in Amér, and not just his heart . . . I mean . . .

ROMY *(Embarrassed)*: Mamá . . .

TOMMY: Amér is not a flower and neither was Father.

MILLIE: But maybe flowers have something to teach us about Lorenzo and Amér *(To Doctor Castillo)* —Cells do have memory? Right, Doctor?

DOCTOR CASTILLO: Sure, they have hereditary information.

MILLIE: That's my point, Tommy. I was told that I sang before I was able to speak.

TOMMY: But music has always been all around you.

MILLIE: That's what I'm trying to say. Everybody in my family sang and we always found ways to express ourselves through song. My father, who was American, was a tenor. And my mother, who was from Spain, sang, and so did all my aunts and uncles.

TOMMY: I don't sing. And Amér is not going to become a songwriter or a conductor, like Father.

IMANOL: I hope not. *(Winks at his brother, patting his thigh)*

DOCTOR CASTILLO: But of course not.

MILLIE: But, Doctor, you do understand what I'm referring to, right?

DOCTOR CASTILLO: Yes, but not what you're suggesting. The word "cell" derives from the Latin "cellula," meaning "small chamber." One could say that a cell is like a music note, right? Let's say . . . And I'm not a good singer. But we have a note like . . . *(Sings note)* Deee . . . We add another note . . . daaa . . . we mix them . . . de da de da daaa . . . de da dee . . . when all these music notes are played together you have a full concerto.

MILLIE: So the cells carry with them memory.

DOCTOR CASTILLO: Sure, certain fragments of intelligence and memory.

MILLIE: Then it must be memories that belonged to my husband.

TOMMY: Mother, you are going too far. He's not talking about those types of memories.

MILLIE: What's your opinion, Doctor?

DOCTOR CASTILLO: There are certain ethical issues concerning this matter.

MILLIE: But we're not at a laboratory talking about these things.

DOCTOR CASTILLO: Yes, but you're suggesting . . . Please, let us deviate from the subject at hand. I believe you are putting me in a difficult position. And I cannot give you an answer that might be unscientific.

AMÉR *(Raising his hand)*: Everything she says makes sense to me. I . . . I feel different.

IMANOL: Of course you feel different. You're starting to feel healthy again.

AMÉR: Can I share something with them, Doctor?

DOCTOR CASTILLO: It's up to you.

AMÉR: The other day I had . . . *(Clears his throat)* I felt a great desire . . . and this has happened to me a few times . . . but I had the desire to listen to music . . . to go to a concert.

MILLIE *(Calmly)*: A concert.

AMÉR: Yes, we bought a ticket and went to listen to an orchestra . . .

MILLIE: And what did you listen to?

AMÉR: Mahler.

MILLIE: Which piece, Amér?

AMÉR: One of the symphonies. *Symphony Number 3.*

MILLIE: And what did you think?

IMANOL: I'm not much of a music lover, but I became very emotional when I noticed how moved he was by the music.

AMÉR: For me it was . . . how can I explain? . . . I felt . . . at one point I had tears in my eyes, and not from sadness, but from joy.

IMANOL: I got all choked up when I saw him cry.

MILLIE: Lorenzo loved Mahler and he played much of his music. *(To Doctor Castillo)* May I say that?

DOCTOR CASTILLO: No, you shouldn't.

AMÉR: Please, after what I have confessed, I don't want you to think that I'm no longer myself.

DOCTOR CASTILLO: But of course not. —Well, I'm afraid it's getting late, and I won't be able to join you for dinner.

MILLIE: Please, don't go, Doctor. Don't go, please.

DOCTOR CASTILLO: I would like very much to stay, but I have work to do.

MILLIE: But you must dine at some point.

DOCTOR CASTILLO: I'm afraid you don't know much about a doctor's life.

MILLIE: But you must eat like everyone else, and sleep like everyone else, and also do nothing.

DOCTOR CASTILLO: Well, if you put it that way and with that smile . . . Let me check my cell phone. *(Takes the phone out of his pocket and checks for messages)* I don't have any calls. No, no one's calling me. Looks like nobody needs a doctor. I don't have any messages. Strange! Well, in this case we use the mechanism that rewinds the cassette tapes, and I do a rewind. *(Walks backward to the place where he was)* I retrace my footsteps, and you see, nothing has happened. Everything is just like before. Ms. Marcel just convinced me to stay for dinner. *(Extracts a handkerchief from his pocket and dries his forehead)* What a relief! What were we talking about?

MILLIE: We were talking about Amér.

DOCTOR CASTILLO: Yes, we were talking about Amér. I'm glad you're here.

(He suddenly feels dizzy.)

How strange! Suddenly, I don't know . . .
MILLIE: Are you all right, Doctor?
DOCTOR CASTILLO: Yes . . . yes . . . I'm well . . . I just.
MILLIE: Would you like to sit down?
DOCTOR CASTILLO: Yes . . . No . . . Okay . . .

(Amér and Imanol help him sit in a chair.)

MILLIE: You want some water?
DOCTOR CASTILLO: No thanks.

(Doctor Castillo shakes his head to get out of the stupor. Millie sits next to him and takes his hand.)

MILLIE: Do you feel better?
DOCTOR CASTILLO: Yes, I'm okay. I'm well. For a moment . . .

(Suddenly, he breaks into laughter and two tears of joy escape from his eyes. He looks at all of them, as if seeing them in a new light.)

Everything seems so clear to me. So limpid. Suddenly, I thought I felt tired of not living.

(All of them laugh.)

MILLIE: But how can that be, Doctor?
DOCTOR CASTILLO: Yes, I'm tired because I think nothing has ever happened in my life.

MILLIE: And yet you have accomplished so much.

DOCTOR CASTILLO: Yes, I earn my bread by replacing hearts. I make someone like Amér have a second chance in life. I tell my patients that life and a person's age should be counted in days and not years. This way, we would feel that we gain more from time. —Let's see, if we were to do that, Amér would be . . . *(Whispers as he multiplies the result)* . . . more than eight thousand days old . . . As for me, I'd be . . . *(Whispers again)* Ugh, I'd have a biblical age. —In all honesty, I suffer from a good malady. I worry about others and I never do anything for myself. I'm a frustrated musician. —Oh! What a dinner conversation, and we haven't even sat down at the table! Maybe you'd prefer if I didn't stay.

MILLIE: But of course. Let's go to the dining room.

(Millie, Amér, Imanol and Doctor Castillo go out.)

TOMMY: What do you think of all this?

ROMY: It was her idea to have this gathering.

TOMMY: What do you think of the boy?

ROMY: He's sweet.

TOMMY *(Shrugs his shoulders)*: I think he's miserable. Does he remind you of Dad?

ROMY: Not at all.

TOMMY: Well, Mother seems to think so . . .

ROMY: Mother is needy.

TOMMY: And you aren't?

ROMY: My father wasn't my husband.

TOMMY: Everyone was in love with Father.

(Millie and Amér reenter.)

MILLIE: Romy, help Dina in the kitchen with the risotto. She doesn't know how to cook it.

ROMY: And neither do I.

MILLIE: I'll go help you in a bit. Tommy, give the men something to drink.

TOMMY: Yes, Sergeant.

(Tommy and Romy exit.)

MILLIE: Amér, let's talk. Don't be frightened by what I said before. That was not my intention.

AMÉR: I'm not frightened.

MILLIE *(Smiling)*: I apologize if I've been too forward.

AMÉR: You don't have to apologize.

MILLIE: I don't know what happened to me when I heard you existed, after you answered my letter. I don't know what struck me. I don't really know what the answer is.

(She walks, wanders through the room.)

Everything in life is always threatening to fade out or take other forms. A leaf. A grain of sand. Everything follows the harvest of its efforts and its end. But now you're here, before me, before everything, and you would still be here if I were to close my eyes and open them again.

AMÉR: But . . . I'm . . . I'm not him . . . You know that, right? I'm not Lorenzo.

MILLIE *(Smiling, lowering her eyes)*: Don't worry. I know that. And yet you are here because of him. And he's here because of you.

AMÉR: I . . . I just think it's important to draw a distinction.

MILLIE: And I do. I do. Even though I seem to be carried away by the sight of you.

61

AMÉR: I'm just a simple man. Believe me . . . if I were a magician . . .

MILLIE: I never liked magicians. To me they are liars. —I'd like for you to feel . . . that you're part of this family.

AMÉR: But we hardly know each other. I'm practically a stranger.

MILLIE *(Smiles)*: You don't have to be. You stand for life. And life is no stranger. —Let's join the others.

(She turns as if to go, as if to be followed by him, but he doesn't move.)

AMÉR: Señora Marcel. *(She turns back to him)* Was he very famous?

MILLIE: He was at the height of his powers when he left us.

AMÉR: Was he very passionate about music?

MILLIE: You would have to listen to his compositions.

AMÉR: What did he look like?

MILLIE: I can show you pictures. He was very tall, elegant, radiant. He was an insatiable collector, but he was also extremely generous. He would waive his fee to give public concerts.

AMÉR: And you were together for many years.

MILLIE: He was probably your age when we met.

AMÉR: Here?

MILLIE: No, in Germany.

(Pause. She fixes her eyes on him.)

—Our intentions to have you be part of our lives are noble. I want you to visit me now and then. No. Come visit me every day. We could go for walks, go to concerts, movies, theaters. We could go to restaurants, have different meals, sit in cafés.

AMÉR: Like you did with Lorenzo?

(Romy enters.)

ROMY: Mamá, I don't know when to add the clams.
MILLIE: Is the rice done?
ROMY: I don't know. I hope I didn't overcook it.
MILLIE: I'll go see. *(Turns to Amér)* It is because of you we
    have begun to live again. It's because of you that we are
    united again. All of this is new to us; the same way we
    are new to you. Tommy will seem less welcoming because
    he's afraid; he's cynical about life. But deep inside he's
    a sensitive and good man. He'll deny the need to have
    you here in this house . . . Forgive him if he might seem
    angry. He is . . . what's the word? Guarded . . . He's per-
    haps a little bitter in the way he expresses himself . . . or
    childish. But don't judge him. Now you're here.

*(Romy looks at Millie, trying to understand what she
wants from Amér. She moves closer to him.)*

And this is a new beginning.

(Millie goes into the kitchen. Romy stays with Amér.)

ROMY: Hanging in there?
AMÉR: Yes, I'm fine.
ROMY: What did Mother put you through?
AMÉR: She was just talking.
ROMY: About Father, of course. He seems to be her only sub-
    ject of conversation.
AMÉR: Yes, she was talking about him.
ROMY: Positive things, of course.
AMÉR: Yes, you can say that. —I like your tattoo.

ROMY: Thank you. Do you also have one?

AMÉR: No.

ROMY: But you have a scar.

AMÉR: And that counts as a tattoo?

ROMY: No. But they have stories just like tattoos.

AMÉR *(Smiling)*: Sad stories.

ROMY: Of course. You can almost decipher the memory of the pain and the moment when the skin yielded itself to the wound. I work at a tattoo shop on Washington Avenue. It's called Deviant Ink. I'm there to cover shoulders, abdomens and scars with my designs. I'm known for my butterfly tattoos and rose tattoos. Yesterday I started a tattoo of a panther on a man who's visiting from Amsterdam. We get all kinds of people at the shop. I think a tree would look interesting on your scar.

AMÉR: An apple tree?

ROMY: An ancient tree.

AMÉR: How about a coconut tree with monkeys?

(They laugh.)

ROMY: You would have to go to the Lady Alice Tattoo Shop for that, or Pretty in Ink. They do silly tattoos. We are serious at Deviant Ink.

(They laugh some more.)

AMÉR: I liked the letter you sent me. I do know how to ride bicycles. Your mother also told me about you in one of the letters she sent me. She told me you're expecting.

ROMY: Yes, as we speak I am making a pair of little hands, two shoulders, two feet, two eyebrows, two eyes and a mouth.

AMÉR: And it's not a tattoo.

ROMY *(Laughs)*: No, it's not a tattoo.

(Romy takes out a cigarette.)

You smoke?

AMÉR: Please don't. You shouldn't.

ROMY: I know . . . I know . . . the baby. I only take a puff.

AMÉR: It's still a puff of smoke.

ROMY: Relax. I like the thrill of lighting one for the sake of lighting it. But don't worry. I'll settle for a lollypop. *(Puts out the cigarette and pulls out a lollypop)* Now I've become boring and dull.

AMÉR: Me too. I feel like I just grow inwards and I've become introspective and wistful. I spend a lot of time by myself, thinking, worrying.

ROMY: Worrying about what?

AMÉR: I guess the responsibility of my good health weighs on me. —Do you think about these things too? I mean, now that you're . . .

ROMY: Yes, too much. Especially now that I'm going to have a baby. I'm going to call her Nadine, which means "hope" in Russian. I want the maternity doctor who is Creole to greet her in French when she's born, "Bienvenue au monde, ma chéri." And I want a Portuguese nurse to say, "Bem-vindo ao mundo, meu querida." *(She laughs full of excitement)* I never want her to think that she is my misfortune, because I'll be a single mother. On the contrary, I want her to know that she's a blessing in my life.

(Imanol comes in with a drink in his hand.)

IMANOL: Excuse me. Millie told me to come get you.

AMÉR: We're coming.

ROMY: I'm sure dinner's not ready.

AMÉR: I don't want her to think that we're rude.

ROMY: Don't worry . . .

IMANOL: Still, I should tell her . . .

ROMY: It's all right. Stay.

IMANOL: Well, if you say so . . .

ROMY: It's hard to be back home after years of living by myself.

IMANOL AND AMÉR *(At the same time)*: And why did you . . . ?

AMÉR: And why did you come back?

ROMY: The baby brought me back. *(Touches her belly)* I am indebted to my mom for everything she's done for me and for the safety she offers me.

IMANOL AND AMÉR *(At the same time)*: We also owe . . .

IMANOL: We also owe a lot to our parents. They sold their home to help with Amér's medical expenses, and now they live with our grandparents.

ROMY: And here I am, always complaining.

IMANOL: You're not the only one. I sometimes go to the sea full of complaints. Why is this happening to me? Why is that happening to me? Why is everything happening to me? And I ask myself, why? Why? And when I look at the blue water, and I see that the sea never laments, that's when I put an end to all my complaints and end the argument.

(Tommy enters.)

TOMMY: Mamá wants you to come join us.

ROMY: We'll be there in a minute.

AMÉR: You go, Imanol, and tell her we're coming.

(Imanol exits. Tommy pretends to leave, but remains at a distance, listening to the conversation.)

ROMY: Do you want to join them?

AMÉR: No, I'd much rather talk to you.

ROMY: My mother and I had a little contest in which we would guess the most things about you.

AMÉR: And did I disappoint you?

ROMY: Not really . . . I imagined you to be I don't know . . .
older and a tad unhappy. I thought you'd be pale and
wan . . . Mother gave you different names, but I always
thought you'd be a John . . .

AMÉR: John and not Juan? Juan and not José? Juan and not
Juaquín?

ROMY *(Laughs)*: No, just John . . . John the enigmatic . . . John
the mysterious.

AMÉR: Your mother believes that some of your father's qualities
have been passed on to me. Do you believe that as well?

ROMY: I don't think so. And if they were, you should try to
break the mold.

(They both laugh.)

AMÉR: Tell me more about him.

ROMY: He wanted a reflection of himself in us, as if we had to
obey his blood. But I'd much rather if you talked about
yourself. I'd much rather know you.

(Tommy interrupts the conversation.)

TOMMY: You should tell him more about papí.

ROMY: Tell him what, Tommy!

TOMMY: Tell him what he was like.

ROMY: Tommy, this is not the time.

TOMMY *(To Amér)*: What is it you'd like to know?

AMÉR: I . . . I . . . really . . . it's not important.

TOMMY: Our father wasn't the best man.

ROMY: I'm going to call Mother.

TOMMY: Call her. Call her. *(In a loud voice to his mother)*
Mamá! Perhaps she'll agree with me this time, and admit
once and for all that he was a despicable man.

ROMY: Tommy.

TOMMY: Go call her. *(To Amér)* We never knew the love of a father. He never cared for her or me. He only cared for himself. He was cold, sadistic, fault-finding and extremely selfish.

ROMY: Tommy, please.

TOMMY: He was sensitive . . . yes he was . . . about his music . . . to the point of being effeminate. And yet he wasn't gay. On the contrary, he made use of his delicate nature and his power as a composer to get the attention of the ladies at the concert halls. *(In a loud voice so that his mother can hear him)* Did you hear that, Mother?

ROMY: Tommy, stop.

TOMMY *(To Amér)*: We grew up with our Aunt Magda, who was childless, but saw us as her own children.

ROMY: Tommy, please . . .

(Romy grabs Tommy by the arm to take him outside.)

Excuse me a moment.

(They exit. Imanol enters. He approaches Amér.)

IMANOL: What are we doing here?

AMÉR: Suddenly, I don't know.

IMANOL: What did we get ourselves into?

AMÉR: I do not know.

IMANOL: They're a little crazy, aren't they? Were they fighting?

AMÉR: The brother . . . I do not know . . . Maybe he has a split personality.

IMANOL: Should we go?

AMÉR: We can't leave.

IMANOL: And the sister, what's going on with her?

AMÉR: She wants to paint a tattoo on my chest.

IMANOL: So fast?

AMÉR: Yes, she wants it to be a tree.

IMANOL: So you beat me to it.

AMÉR: No, not so fast. Can we stay for a while longer?

IMANOL: And do what? I want to go now.

AMÉR: Let's make an effort and get to know them.

IMANOL: Does the house seem familiar to you?

AMÉR: Why are you asking me that?

IMANOL: Just wondering. Any memories? Of the furniture? Of the father's studio?

AMÉR: No, not at all. But it's a beautiful home. And so is the daughter.

(Romy and Tommy enter.)

ROMY: Sorry about that. My brother and I needed to have a little chat.

TOMMY: It's done. Now everything is in order. My sister doesn't like me to give my opinion of my father.

(Millie enters with a cocktail in her hand, accompanied by Doctor Castillo.)

MILLIE: Why were you yelling?

TOMMY: I was talking about your husband.

MILLIE: Oh yes! What about Lorenzo?

TOMMY: I was acquainting them with Daddy. The love of your life.

MILLIE: Yes, he was.

TOMMY: And you were always his victim, the lamb on the path to be sacrificed.

MILLIE *(With irony)*: As you can see, Tommy likes to indulge in irony and dismiss simple explanations about life and people.

TOMMY: Do I, Mother?

MILLIE: As a child, imagination was his ruling faculty. Isn't that right, Romy? He liked to deform reality. He was a boy who liked to invent strange rites and games. I even remember one day, when I was rehearsing, he was doing schoolwork, making strange drawings, chewing on his pencil, mooning for hours. And I thought to myself, "What in the world is going through his head?"

TOMMY: I was probably thinking of killing someone.

MILLIE *(With irony)*: Oh, that's not a nice thing to say. What were you reading then, Son?

TOMMY: Probably *Hamlet*. But Hamlet wanted to kill his stepfather and not his own dad.

MILLIE *(To Amér)*: A bourbon, Amér? Gin? A martini? A tequila? A cocktail of some sort?

AMÉR: I'm not supposed to drink.

MILLIE: Oh, just a tiny bit. We'll pretend that Doctor Castillo and your brother don't see you.

DOCTOR CASTILLO: I have eyes everywhere, Ms. Marcel, even when I'm off duty.

IMANOL: A little sip won't hurt you.

AMÉR: That's okay, señora. I'm not going to drink. Thank you.

MILLIE: I'm not supposed to drink either. But today I'm going to stop supposing. *(Takes a swig from her cocktail)* To you, and you, and you. To all. Today we are celebrating these two young men who have joined our family.

(She downs her whole cocktail.)

Make me another drink!

ROMY: No, Mother.

MILLIE: I want another drink.

ROMY: Everything in moderation, Mother.

MILLIE: All right, then only one more.

TOMMY: Bourbon is not your best friend, Mother.

MILLIE: Who says? I can handle a bottle of bourbon; it is the bottle of bourbon that can't handle me.

TOMMY: You start getting a little lost in a cloud. Or to be even more precise, you get lost in a storm.

MILLIE: Oh stop wearing that funereal expression and be happy.

TOMMY: I am happy. *(Raising his glass)* To you, Mother. To you, Amér and Imanol. My sister. And to Father. To my father, who is beyond any words that we could say about him. He still lives in the music he composed, the songs he wrote. He slept on the left side of bed with my mother. He . . . he was successful at everything he did, but perhaps he was really unhappy with our mother.

MILLIE: I don't know what you're saying.

TOMMY: Yes, of course. You'd probably never admit to this. *(To the rest)* Our mother . . . she was so busy trying to hold on to Dad and his concerts, and her own career as a singer, that sometimes she'd forget she had children.

MILLIE: Tommy, have some respect, for God's sake.

TOMMY: Respect for whom? For him? For you? What I want to know is who's going to pay for the damage, Mother? And I'm not talking about money . . . monetary compensation. I don't want money. Our father had insurance for everything, against all acts of nature: floods, hurricanes, earthquakes, fires, blizzards . . . but the old man had no insurance to cover his own actions, his own absence in my life.

ROMY: Tommy, don't make this about you.

TOMMY: You're right. It's not about me. It's about this innocent man that our mother is bringing into our family.

IMANOL: Ms. Marcel, I'm afraid we're going to have to leave. Do you want to leave, Amér?

AMÉR: Yes, let's go.

TOMMY: What are you doing? Where are you taking him? She wants him to join the family, right? And you as well. *(To Millie)* You brought him here, didn't you?

DOCTOR CASTILLO: No, I brought him here.

AMÉR: We went through all the protocols so we could meet. But I never thought . . .

TOMMY: Okay . . . okay . . . so let's start with a clean slate. *(To Millie)* What is it that you want from Amér? To resuscitate your blind worship of Lorenzo through him? *(Points to Amér)*

MILLIE: No, I don't want to resuscitate anybody.

TOMMY: Then what do you want, Mother? To find his double? To catch reflections of him in Amér?

MILLIE: STOP THIS NONSENSE!

TOMMY: Just stop this blindness and face the truth!

MILLIE: You see. It's all in his head.

TOMMY: No, damn your blind eyes!

DOCTOR CASTILLO: Tommy, show some respect!

IMANOL: Let's go, Amér. Let's go.

(Imanol grabs Amér by the arm.)

MILLIE: Please don't go.

IMANOL: THEN I WISH HE WOULD STOP TALKING THIS WAY!

AMÉR: What were you hoping for, Ms. Marcel, when you brought us here?

MILLIE *(Absentmindedly)*: Hoping for?

AMÉR: Yes, when you asked Doctor Castillo if we could meet.

MILLIE: Well . . . I don't know . . . It goes without saying that I wanted you to know about Lorenzo.

TOMMY: But only the Lorenzo she wishes you to know.

MILLIE: Why would I tell him about any other Lorenzo than the one I loved, the one I married?

TOMMY: You could tell him about his double game.

MILLIE: There was no double game with Lorenzo.

TOMMY: You're lying. He just knew how to play his cards well. *(To Amér)* In public he seemed to be a man who was affectionate, humane, devoted, modest, compassionate, but in private he was reckless, vehement and selfish. And unfaithful to you.

MILLIE: Oh he probably had crushes. We all have crushes. I had my own crushes on other singers that I'd perform with. —But I would stake my life on it that he never had an affair!

TOMMY: How can you say that, Mother? Everyone knew . . .

MILLIE: I made a point of verifying that he had crushes . . . infatuations with certain artists.

(Doctor Castillo's cell phone rings.)

DOCTOR CASTILLO: I'm sorry. This damn phone. Pardon me. I have to go out to answer this call.

(Doctor Castillo exits.)

ROMY: Are you getting overwhelmed, Amér?

AMÉR: Hmm? *(Snapping out of it)* Oh, I'm sorry. I wasn't paying attention. I was thinking of something else.

IMANOL: Do you want to leave?

AMÉR: No, I'm fine. But I think you need to talk.

MILLIE: Please don't. Do not leave.

IMANOL: We should go in a little while. I don't want you to feel uncomfortable.

MILLIE: We were all joking.

TOMMY: Yes, we must eat her food. Mother made dinner. And Mother doesn't make dinner every day. I think she'll be very disappointed if you leave. Wouldn't you be, Mother?

MILLIE: I'll be disappointed if you continue with all this non-sense you're talking about. Let's just have a peaceful and quiet dinner.

TOMMY *(Stands on a chair)*: I apologize if I'm not good at fam-ily reunions. For those of you who enjoy family gatherings and like to be part of the beehive, I offer my apologies. For those who are happy and don't mind the shackles and chains of this form of slavery, I offer my regrets. Yes, I'm not patriotic. I don't do well in beehives and colonies of ants, in the cozy and easy warmth of a family, nor do I find satisfaction in belonging to a tribe. But today I'm here for you, Mother. Because I love you, Mother. And you made my father's favorite dish for dinner.

MILLIE: I just made what I know how to cook best.

TOMMY: Then I'll make myself pleasant and enjoy your meal with the new members of the family. Let's go!

ROMY: Why are you doing this, Tommy?

TOMMY: Because I might never have the chance to have Moth-er's food again.

ROMY *(Rolls her eyes)*: Why? Are you planning to kill yourself?

TOMMY: No, that would be an easy way out. *(To Amér)* —How about if we set the table right here, Mother? *(He illus-trates a dining room table)* We serve wine. *(To Millie)* The meal is served. And after a few bites of the food, we talk about the other Lorenzo. Because it's strange that an artistic and intelligent woman like you has given up on your career to grieve over a man, a man who used to have more than infatuations with young women.

MILLIE: I'm afraid these are things one doesn't talk about at a table.

TOMMY: Care to join me in the billiards room, where coffee would be served, and we could have more of a private conversation? *(He takes Amér by the arm)*

AMÉR: Is this why you asked me to come here, to play with me?

TOMMY: A question, just between the two of us—besides music, have you developed a passion for photography?

AMÉR: No, I can't say that I have.

IMANOL: He takes pictures with his phone, and that's all . . .

TOMMY: Father had a passion for photography. He liked taking photos of us when we were kids. He expressed his affection for us by way of the lens.

MILLIE: You make it sound as if he only cared for you from a distance.

TOMMY: Please don't disturb us.

MILLIE: You father even composed lullabies for you and Romy.

ROMY: Mother, would it not be easier to simply let him finish what he's trying to tell Amér?

MILLIE: No, he exaggerates reality.

TOMMY: Let's do something. Do you have your cell phone with you?

AMÉR: Yes, I do.

TOMMY: Let me call you.

AMÉR: But I'm here.

TOMMY: Give me your number. I'll call you. *(To Millie)* And don't tell me there are things that should not be discussed over the phone.

MILLIE: This is absurd!

TOMMY: Give me your number.

AMÉR: 305-421-2168.

(Tommy dials the number.)

TOMMY: 421-2168.

(Amér's phone rings. For a moment he doesn't know what to do. He looks at Millie and Romy. Millie lowers her head in disbelief. Imanol is about to say something, but Amér signals him not to utter a word. The phone continues to ring.

75

*Tommy in a state of embarrassment begins to cry. Ima-
nol looks at Romy. Romy looks at Millie. After a moment,
Amér answers the call.)*

AMÉR: Hello. *(No response)* Do you want to talk? *(No answer)*
I can listen. Hello. Are you there? Can you hear me? *(No
answer)*
IMANOL: Hang up, Amér. Hang up.
AMÉR *(Avoiding Imanol)*: Hello. I don't understand. I'm here.
Do you hear me? Can I help you?

(Tommy's game has turned dangerously dark.)

TOMMY: I don't know if you can.
AMÉR: But you wanted to call me.
TOMMY: I did.
AMÉR: And you wanted for me to listen to you.
TOMMY: Yes.
AMÉR: Do you still want to talk? You can say anything you
want. You obviously want to tell me something.
TOMMY: No. Not you. Not you. My father.
AMÉR: Is it something you never got to tell him? *(No answer)*
Is it?
TOMMY: Yes.
AMÉR: Then tell him.
TOMMY: Is your heart beating like crazy?
AMÉR: Yes. And yours?
TOMMY: Yes, probably just as fast.
AMÉR: Are you afraid?
TOMMY: Yes. Well, no. Yes. But I'll be fine.
AMÉR: Why is it so difficult?
TOMMY: Because I thought I had the courage. I've rehearsed
this moment in front of the mirror so many times.
AMÉR: I'm nervous as well.

TOMMY: Bring the phone closer to your chest.

(Amér hesitates.)

Do as I tell you, please.

AMÉR: All right.

TOMMY *(Into his cell phone)*: Do you hear me? This is Tommy. Talking to you . . . talking to you in this way is like speaking for the first time after you've been asleep from a coma. You wake up to the present and yet you're still many years behind, where you stayed silent and frozen in time. Do you understand what I'm saying? You must know. Did you know that Mother made me her confidant when you were alive? When you had these so-called "crushes"? That's why she sent me with you when you were on tour with your orchestra?

MILLIE: Don't say those things, Tommy.

TOMMY *(To Millie)*: Yes, you did, Mother.

MILLIE: I thought I was helping you. You wanted to be a musician.

ROMY: Let him say what he needs to say, Mother.

TOMMY *(Into his phone)*: It was all a plan so you wouldn't meet any women and bring them back to the hotel.

MILLIE: That's a lie. I wanted for you to learn how to travel . . . how to be in an orchestra.

ROMY: Let him talk!

TOMMY: Remember the cello player in your orchestra? Paolo Carli? Remember that day you left me with him? Paolo said he would look after me while you went out to dinner with Maria Berlotti. *(To Millie)* Do you remember Berlotti, Mother?

MILLIE: I do.

TOMMY: Father had an affair with her, didn't he?

MILLIE: Yes, he had a little story with Berlotti.

TOMMY *(Yelling into his phone)*: See, she admits she knew about it. —So that night, that night, when you left me with Paolo Carli. Paolo said he would teach me how to play the cello. And he did. But do you know how he did it? He started by teaching me how to change the pitch of the strings by turning the pegs. Then he told me to sit down, and placed the cello between my legs. Then he whispered into my ear how to hold it as if it were the body of a woman. Then he reached over me and guided my hands so I'd familiarize myself with the cello's neck and the rest of its body. That's when his breath brushed against my neck, as he embraced me, holding me as if I were also a cello, gliding his hands down my body. And I sat there, eyes closed, frozen, wanting him to stop, to stop . . . but he continued . . . he went on, telling me that we could both love this body of wood, making it sing, discovering the music of Bach and Boccherini. And all I could hear was dissonant music as his touch spread like a forest fire all over my body. From then on, the classes continued every time Mother would send me to accompany you on your tours. I used to beg her not to force me to go.

I pleaded, "Mother, please, don't send me on the tours. Don't send me." And I was so afraid to tell you about those lessons, because I was afraid of losing the music.

IMANOL: Hang up! Hang up!

(Imanol takes Amér's phone from him.)

We're leaving! We're leaving! Come on, let's go. *(To Amér)* They're using you. *(To Millie)* You don't need to put him through this. He's not your husband. *(To Tommy)* And he's not your father. And he's not a puppet!

AMÉR: Hold on! Hold on!

IMANOL: Let's go. It's not fair what they're putting you through.
AMÉR: It's okay, Imanol. He just needed to talk.
IMANOL: Then let him see a shrink. —Let's go.
MILLIE: Can't you have some compassion?
IMANOL: Compassion? For whom? For what? Your son's confession has nothing to do with my brother. You can't expect him to take all this rubbish you're throwing at him.
ROMY: He's right, Mother.

(Slight pause.)

IMANOL: Of course, I'm damn right! I'm going to call Doctor Castillo to tell him what's going on.
TOMMY: Yes, call him and tell him to come back.
MILLIE: I'm so confused . . . all of this . . . all of this . . . to hear Tommy . . . to hear him. Please. Let us talk this through. Everything was going so well.
TOMMY: Nothing was going well. Nothing.
MILLIE: Yes . . . yes . . . everything was going well. We were beginning to know Amér.
IMANOL: You weren't interested in knowing him.
MILLIE: Of course I was. I just don't know why you had to bring that up, Tommy. Why bring it up now? . . . Why now?
TOMMY: Because the past isn't just the passed by, it persists! It stays! It festers!
MILLIE: But you could've told me when it happened. I would've stopped it. Why didn't you tell me then?
TOMMY: Because you never listen! You never listen. Because you are notorious for being out of touch with reality, because in actual life you don't want to know about this, and now much less, because you're always immersed in your world of music and opera, because you prefer to live on the stage and stand in your own little fake light and

suffer the exquisite agony of Salome, Mimi and Desde-
mona. Because deep inside, you always wanted Romy
and me to be crushed and wounded, just like you were
humiliated by Daddy.

(Beat.)

MILLIE: Come here. Would you let me hug you?
TOMMY: No. No, Mother. We are not doing a revival of your
own exquisite agony tonight, even though we have all the
players. Even a young man has joined us tonight, so we
can enact it all over again for you.

(Imanol grabs Amér by the arm and pulls him.)

IMANOL: Let's go. Let's go. He's not an actor.
AMÉR: Let go of me!
IMANOL: All of this is humiliating.
AMÉR: LEAVE ME ALONE!

(Imanol and Amér struggle with each other.)

IMANOL: Let's go, I said!
AMÉR: I told you! I told you I don't want to leave!
IMANOL: I don't want you here. You're not a dead man. Can't
you see what they're doing to you?
MILLIE: Let go of him!
ROMY: What are you doing? . . . Leave him alone.
TOMMY: . . . Let him take him . . .
IMANOL: Come . . . come on . . . this has nothing to do with
you. Let's go . . .
AMÉR: Leave me alone . . .
ROMY: Let go of him!
IMANOL: Stay out of this . . .

(Romy manages to separate the brothers.)

ROMY: LET GO OF HIM!

IMANOL *(After a pause)*: Let him do whatever he wants. Let
him stay if he wants. I'm leaving. *(To Amér)* I'll wait for
you in the car.

(Imanol storms out. Silence.)

MILLIE: What just happened? Only two minutes ago we were
fine. We were trying to get to know each other. We were
about to serve dinner. *(To Tommy)* Now everything has
been spoiled.

TOMMY: You can't blame me.

ROMY: You didn't have to go into that whole rant! Didn't you
hear yourself? You always want to make everything about
you. Do you think you're the only one who has suffered?
Do you think you're the only one who suffers? I've always
known your pain. And I always felt sorry for you when you
used to cry on my shoulder, because the fear you felt—
the fear that we are alone—I used to feel it as well. That
doubt . . . no, it's not doubt . . . that sense of desolation
used to lash out at me, when you were in one part of the
world with Dad and I was in another with Mother. I also
suffered like you did and never said anything, because
the one who suffers hides it, and keeps quiet about it.
I learned this from you, from Mother, from myself.

TOMMY: So is it my fault? Is it? Do you want me to feel guilty?

ROMY: Yes, it's your fault! Because if you were still suffering,
you wouldn't say anything.

TOMMY: So you want me to feel guilty? Do you think I feel
better now that I've talked about it? Do you think Father
heard me? Did I hear myself?

ROMY: I don't know.

TOMMY: Me neither. Did I sound like a child? Did I? Maybe I made a mistake. Because it might be too late to let go of that child. *(To Millie)* Was I awful, mamá? I gave a bad performance, right?

MILLIE: No, you did well.

TOMMY: I'm glad.

(Tommy breaks down crying. Amér goes to Tommy and tries to console him.)

AMÉR: Calm yourself, Tommy.

TOMMY: Don't you touch me!

AMÉR: Tommy, I know you're hurt.

(Tommy grabs Amér by his shirt. He is about to punch him.)

TOMMY: What the hell do you know? What the hell do you know about me?!

(Tommy, full of rage, remains frozen with his fist pointed at Amér.)

ROMY: Don't you dare hit him!

MILLIE: Enough! Get away from him!

TOMMY: No, you're already dead.

(Millie goes to Tommy.)

MILLIE: Tommy, calm down. Calm down. Enough of that . . . come . . . come . . . it's over . . . it's over . . . forgive me, Son . . . forgive me . . .

(Millie manages to get Tommy away from Amér. Romy goes to Amér and hugs him.
  Imanol enters.)

IMANOL: Let's go, Amér. *(To the family)* I told Doctor Castillo what's going on. *(To Amér)* Come on. He told me to take you home.

ROMY: Do you want to stay? I'll take you back in my car.

IMANOL: He's not going to stay. I'm responsible for him.

ROMY: Stay. You can stay over. We can stay in the guest room. We can go for a walk and get some fresh air. I'll take you back in the morning after we have breakfast.

IMANOL: He's not staying. *(Grabs his brother by the arm)* We both work tomorrow. He needs a good rest and I'm afraid he won't rest here. —Let's go.

MILLIE: Please. Don't take him like that.

IMANOL: We need to go now.

MILLIE: Let me at least say goodbye.

(Millie goes to Amér.)

We made a mistake. We should've been more prepared to meet you. We . . . We met you with expectations instead of amiability. We . . . We tormented you with our grievances. I am so sorry. Perhaps we should've waited.

AMÉR: Perhaps I should've waited to meet you as well and been better prepared.

ROMY: You must think we are monsters.

AMÉR: No. On the contrary, I don't understand why I'm here. And yet I do. I do, without understanding it. Maybe there is something to understand, but I don't want to question it.

ROMY: Please, come back.

AMÉR: Thank you. If you want, you can visit me as well. *(Includes Imanol)* The two of us. Or you can come visit me at the aquarium store where I work, until I go back to my country. *(Playfully)* And if you do go, there you'll be able to see all the variety of fish that we sell. You know, fish are remarkable creatures. They're known to remember faces.

The ones at my store know me. They gather on one side of the fish tank when they see me, because they know I take care of them. It's curious. If you stare at them for some time, they can help you calm the heart. I know they help me. I always feel delighted when I look at them. And I feel more accepting. And with acceptance comes patience with things that are difficult for me to comprehend. And I think it helps me not to reject what's been given to me.

(Amér brings his hand to his heart.
He turns to go and heads for the door, followed by Imanol.)

ROMY: Amér. We'd like to get to know you. I mean, who you really are. At least I do. And also, I'm sure I can do something . . . that is . . . with your scar . . . at least I can cover it with the figure of a tree or a butterfly or a fish.
AMÉR: Of course.

(Amér and Imanol exit.
The family stays still, feeling the absence of the brothers, and perhaps the absence of their father.
Stillness.
Romy turns away from her family.)

ROMY: What will he think of us? What could he be saying? What is he talking about with his brother? Where does he live? What does he do in the evening? We didn't find out anything about him. —Where did we get lost? Where did we lose him? How do we get him to come back? Do you think he suffers?
TOMMY: He suffers, as we all suffer, without saying anything.
ROMY: There should be an ink that doesn't cover things, but erases them.

But nothing is erased. Nothing. Nothing. Not even the will of death.

(Doctor Castillo enters.)

DOCTOR CASTILLO: I am sorry. I was talking to a patient. —Imanol told me . . .

ROMY: They're gone.

DOCTOR CASTILLO: I just saw them and I said goodbye.

ROMY: It's late. *(She exits)*

DOCTOR CASTILLO: But what happened? Imanol told me . . .

TOMMY: Nothing happened, Doctor. Nothing ever happens. I was just talking about my father. Amér listened to me. My mother got upset. My sister got irritated and Imanol got angry. Now everyone hates me. That's all. *(He goes out)*

MILLIE: It must be difficult.

DOCTOR CASTILLO: What do you mean?

MILLIE *(Looks into the distance)*: Dealing with hearts.

DOCTOR CASTILLO: Yes, it's the most delicate and intimate thing in the human being.

MILLIE: How many stones do you need to kill someone? One, two, three? And to finish him off, how many stones? One? Yes, it has to be one stone, if it takes one single color to paint blood. And what death is the real one, Doctor? The physical one? Or is it the death that comes when you're forgotten? Or the one that comes when you're remembered but you feel helpless because you can't really mend a memory?

DOCTOR CASTILLO: Why are you saying these things?

MILLIE: Because if memories can't be mended, we managed to use one stone to kill off Lorenzo.

DOCTOR CASTILLO: And all this happened when I was gone.

MILLIE: Yes.

DOCTOR CASTILLO: And Amér is okay?

MILLIE: We didn't get to know him. We didn't make the effort to treat him as he deserves, and that is not fair.

DOCTOR CASTILLO: Then there was some damage.

MILLIE: I'm sure there was. But it's wrong to make him carry the pain of others.

DOCTOR CASTILLO: We can't do anything about it. He has been given a heart to continue living, and to continue feeling what others have felt.

Because the heart not only beats to the forward rhythm of time. The heart also beats toward the past, in silence, resonating with all that was, with all those who were before us, before the world; when it began to be heard in the imagination of God, to the sound of the first steps of men and women, and the rumor of leaves and the wind . . .

(He stands very close to Millie) May I? *(He takes her hand)* The heart also guards its fragility, and gives no sign of its possible leap and fall. Right now, at this moment, in front of you, my heart has become like a child, like a restless playful dog before your eyes.

(Silence.

He looks at her and smiles. She allows herself to embrace the look in his eyes.)

MILLIE: Guard your heart the way I couldn't guard mine.

(She moves away from him and looks into the distance.)

END OF PLAY

Nilo Cruz is a Cuban-American playwright whose work has been produced widely across the U.S., including performances with such distinguished companies as Princeton's McCarter Theatre Center, New York's Public Theater, and Manhattan Theatre Club. Internationally, Cruz's plays have been produced in Canada, England, France, Australia, Germany, Belarus, Costa Rica, Colombia, Panama, Ecuador, Japan, Russia, and in cities throughout Spain. In 2003, Cruz became the first Latino to win the Pulitzer Prize for Drama, thanks to his most celebrated work, *Anna in the Tropics*.

Theatre Communications Group would like to offer our special thanks to the Vilcek Foundation for its generous support of the publication of Exquisite Agony *by Nilo Cruz*

THE VILCEK FOUNDATION raises awareness of immigrant contributions in America and fosters appreciation of the arts and sciences. Established in 2000 by Jan and Marica Vilcek, immigrants from the former Czechoslovakia, the foundation's mission was inspired by the couple's respective careers in biomedical science and art history, as well as their appreciation for the opportunities offered to them as newcomers to the United States.

TCG books sponsored by the Vilcek Foundation include:

Appropriate/An Octoroon: Plays, Branden Jacobs-Jenkins
Cost of Living, Martyna Majok
The Detroit Project, Dominique Morisseau
Exquisite Agony, Nilo Cruz
Five Plays, Sam Hunter
The Language Archive and Other Plays, Julia Cho
Miss You Like Hell, Quiara Alegría Hudes and Erin McKeown
Mr. Burns and Other Plays, Anne Washburn

THEATRE COMMUNICATIONS GROUP (TCG), the national organization for the American theatre, promotes the idea of "A Better World for Theatre, and a Better World Because of Theatre." In addition to TCG's numerous services to the theatre field, TCG Books is the nation's largest independent publisher of dramatic literature, with 17 Pulitzer Prizes for Drama on its book list. The book program commits to the life-long career of its playwrights, keeping all of their plays in print. TCG Books' other authors include: Annie Baker, Athol Fugard, David Henry Hwang, Tony Kushner, Donald Margulies, Lynn Nottage, Suzan-Lori Parks, Sarah Ruhl, Stephen Sondheim, and August Wilson, among many others.

Support TCG's work in the theatre field by becoming a member or donor: www.tcg.org

tcg